Becoming Native *to* Win the Natives

Becoming Native to Win the Natives

Cross-Culturally Becoming All Things to All Men

Tabor Laughlin

WIPF & STOCK · Eugene, Oregon

BECOMING NATIVE TO WIN THE NATIVES
Cross-Culturally Becoming All Things to All Men

Copyright © 2016 Tabor Laughlin. All rights reserved. Except for brief quotations in critical publications or reviews, no part of this book may be reproduced in any manner without prior written permission from the publisher. Write: Permissions, Wipf and Stock Publishers, 199 W. 8th Ave., Suite 3, Eugene, OR 97401.

Wipf & Stock
An Imprint of Wipf and Stock Publishers
199 W. 8th Ave., Suite 3
Eugene, OR 97401

www.wipfandstock.com

PAPERBACK ISBN: 978-1-4982-9018-0
HARDCOVER ISBN: 978-1-4982-9020-3

Manufactured in the U.S.A.

To my wife Lynne
And to my daughters Joy and Ann

> "I have become all things to all people so that by all possible means I might save some."
>
> —1 CORINTHIANS 9:22

Contents

Preface | ix

Section I: Principles for Becoming Native to Win the Natives
    1 What's This Book About? | 3
    2 Must Have Humility and Love | 11

Section II: Practically How to Become Native to Win the Natives
    3 Diving into Language | 25
    4 Assimilating into the Local Culture | 37
    5 Appearance to Local Community | 45
    6 Family Life | 52

Section III: What to Take Away from All This?
    7 Final Thoughts | 63

    Bibliography | 71

Preface

FOR CROSS-CULTURAL MINISTRY, WE learn from the apostle Paul: "I have become all things to all men so that *by all possible means I might save some*" (1 Cor 9:22). We can see this displayed in his preaching to the Athenians in Acts 17, how he becomes a local Athenian by relating to them through their culture. Hudson Taylor later lived out this model well in China.

This book first looks at how we are to imitate Christ's love and humility to effectively love the locals we are ministering to. Then the book covers many specific aspects of life abroad and how we can better live like the locals in all of these areas, that some may be saved.

These aspects of following the local life include: diving into language (language learning, volunteering at a local shop/restaurant); assimilating into the local culture (sports, entertainment, holidays, transportation, food and drink); our appearance to the local community (our physical appearance, job, and our integrity in the community); and our family life (kids' education, medical care, outreach as a family, wife's language learning). The book also talks about what to do if you find that you really don't love the local people at all, and also how to objectively analyze the local culture.

Section I

Principles for Becoming Native to Win the Natives

1

What's This Book About?

Introduction

OVER THE NEARLY TEN years that I've been living in China, many Chinese friends and foreign friends alike have told me that I am more like a Chinese person than I am an American. I take that statement as a compliment. It is my intent to fit in as well as possible with the local Chinese, so as to be more effective in reaching them for the gospel, and in some sense to leave behind the identity of the country where I grew up. I've heard it as a reference to Chinese people who act more like an American, that they are called "bananas" (yellow on the outside, white on the inside); maybe that same logic would make me an "egg" (white on the outside, yellow on the inside). I've never heard this terminology used before for someone like me, who has pale white skin on the outside but on the inside is more like an Asian (Chinese) person, but that would be quite an accurate statement to describe my current makeup.

 I don't have any particular gifting in evangelism or preaching. I've never planted a church. Since I first arrived in China over ten years ago, I feel like the Lord has given me grace to dive into the local Chinese culture, language, history, food, entertainment, and customs. I love to soak up as much as possible about this great place. Since I first got off the plane and stepped my first steps on Chinese soil, the Lord has given me a huge heart for the Chinese. Even when first arriving in China, I knew that I would be aiming to reach the Chinese for many years. I also dreaded the day, down the road, when I would have to leave this place. When I first arrived in China, the Lord's grace was on me to enjoy the culture and to soak it up, rather than to complain about it and hate it. For the most part, the Lord's grace has continued to be on me in this regard, to desire to fit in with the Chinese people like Hudson Taylor did so many years ago.

Slightly altering Paul's words from Romans 15:16, I'd say that my ambition is "to be a minister of Christ Jesus to the [Chinese] with the priestly duty of proclaiming the gospel of God, so that the [Chinese] might become an offering acceptable to God, sanctified by the Holy Spirit" (Rom. 15:16). This is my ambition, to minister to the Chinese to help in a small way to present the Chinese people as an acceptable offering, holy and blameless to the Lord. The hope of this book is that you may also be able to do the same thing with those you are ministering to, not only in the context of China, but around the globe. My prayer is that you may be more fruitful in sharing the gospel with others, particularly cross-culturally, and that this book may help you, even a little bit, to become all things to all men, so that you may, by all possible means, save some.

Personal Background

I grew up in the middle of the Bible Belt and Tornado Alley, but was just a cultural Christian growing up. The main event in my life that got me looking towards God in the first place and that brought me to the faith was my mother's genetic disease. It was learning about her disease while I was in high school that got me going to a weekly Bible study and beginning to actually read the Bible on my own for the first time. I felt completely terrified of death and hopeless about life, and I recognized my own sin and weakness. As I thought about the meaning of life and my mother's seemingly quite shortened life—and possibly my own shortened life, as

What's This Book About?

well—the Lord finally brought me from darkness to light during my sophomore year in college. I was studying abroad in England for the year. It was then that I first had genuine repentance that leads to salvation, and the Lord's Spirit inside of me began to change me into his likeness.

Once I became a believer, as I had done much traveling in the United States and overseas when I was younger, it seemed very reasonable to think the Lord may use me overseas upon graduation. Also, the previous summer I had had my first taste of missions, when I spent the whole summer serving for a ministry in Thailand. During that time, the Lord affirmed in my heart that I would be doing missions for my life. This was further confirmed when I returned to my college (Oklahoma State University) for my senior year. I started an international Bible study there, which grew quite a bit. I was able to minister to students from all around the world for that year. This was another way for the Lord to confirm his path for me after graduation.

In 2005 I graduated with a bachelor's degree in Aerospace and Mechanical Engineering from Oklahoma State University. Later, in 2005, I moved to eastern China to minister there and teach at a university. After three years in eastern China leading a missions team, I felt the Lord calling me to western China, where the workers were fewer. Now I have lived in China for over nine years. I met my wife here in China, though we are both from the same city in the United States. We had a daughter here in western China in 2012.

I graduated from Southern Baptist Theological Seminary in Louisville, Kentucky with a master of divinity degree in missions with a concentration in Islamic studies. Nearly five years ago I helped start a small missions organization that focuses on mobilizing missionaries into Northwest China. I am currently president of the organization and am overseeing about twenty workers in three cities in Northwest China. I teach at the top high school in our province.

Principles for Becoming Native to Win the Natives

Paul's Becoming All Things to All Men

This book is about becoming native to win the natives. In thinking about cross-cultural ministry, it is necessary to consider the model of the apostle Paul. Actually, Paul cannot be considered as a completely appropriate model for us who now serve as missionaries. For one thing, Paul never learned a foreign language for the sake of preaching the gospel. He grew up learning both Greek and Hebrew. These were not languages that he attained solely for the purpose of ministry. Everywhere he traveled, the locals would be able to communicate in Greek. There is no mention in the Bible of Paul learning another language, or of Paul ever using a translator to help him preach to the locals. So in regards to learning a foreign language for the purpose of ministry, Paul, as far as we know, never did this.

However, Paul still sets an example for us in other ways. Though he did not preach in any foreign languages, he did strive to be relevant to those with whom he was speaking. The most well known example is when Paul was preaching to the Greeks in Athens in Acts 17. Paul notes to them that they are very religious people (v. 23), then he begins to share with them about the true God (v. 23). He does this by quoting their pagan writings (v. 28–29). Then he tells them that now the time has come when God wants them to repent (v. 30). They must repent because there will be a day of judgment (v. 31). So, in this short sermon Paul is appealing to something that is very familiar to the Athenians, which are their poems about Zeus. He makes a point of contact with the listeners, not in a critical way, but in a way that attracts their attention and shows his concern for them. Then he is able to share with them about the one living God.

We can see the thoughts behind Paul's actions in Athens when we read his words in 1 Corinthians 9:19–22. Paul writes that he becomes a Jew to win the Jews. He becomes one under the law to win those under the law. He becomes like one not under the law to win those not having the law. He becomes weak to win the weak.

Then the conclusion is profound: "I have become all things to all men so that by all possible means I might save some" (1 Cor 9:22).

So, Paul's purpose in becoming all things to all men is so that some may be saved. We can see this displayed in his preaching to the Athenians in Acts 17—how he becomes a local Athenian by relating to them through their culture. And he does this not just for the sake of befriending them, but more importantly so that they may be saved. So, though Paul did not need to learn any foreign languages to preach the gospel to the unreached, we can still learn much from him about cross-cultural ministry. Paul set a ministry paradigm that we are to follow in all contexts, whether at home or abroad. We must relate to those we are ministering to in order that some may be saved.

Hudson Taylor's Example

This is what this book is about—to see practically what it looks like to become like the natives to win the natives. Many of us know the example of Hudson Taylor in the eighteen hundreds, who traveled from England to China as a missionary at the age of twenty-two. He lived in a big city by the sea for a while, congregating mostly with the other foreign missionaries and seeing very little fruit among the locals. But he saw the limitations of looking like a foreigner and acting like a foreigner. Taylor knew that if he acted, talked, and looked like a foreigner as he preached the gospel, then the locals would only understand that gospel as something foreign and would not be able to accept the gospel as something for all peoples.

So Taylor moved into a part of the city that did not have other foreigners living there. He spent all of his time around the local Chinese, and began wearing the traditional Chinese clothes and a traditional Chinese hair braid. When he was totally assimilated into the local culture, his language improved quite rapidly. He was doing missions much differently than the other missionaries. As a result of Taylor's adoption of the Chinese dress and hair braid, he was alienated from the other foreign missionaries in the city. Many of them cut ties with him altogether. They just thought he was a young renegade.

Though he was greatly criticized at the time by the other foreign missionaries for diving into the Chinese culture, his missions approach was undoubtedly quite effective. Because he looked and talked like the locals, and showed great love and concern for them and their culture, the Chinese welcomed Taylor with open arms and took him in as one of their own. As a result, his ministry with the locals became incredibly fruitful. His attitude was what began what would later become fifty years of fruitful service to the Chinese. Hudson Taylor is a great example for us of what it means to heed Paul's words to "become all things to all men to by all means save some."

Balance in Missions

Living like the natives is specifically what this book is focused on. Missions, of course, is not just about living like the locals. It is important in missions not only to live like the locals, but also to build deep relationships with them and to be intentional to share with them the gospel. Paul says, "How can they call on the one they have not believed on?" (Rom 10:14). It is possible to "live like the natives," but to not actually be sharing the gospel or building deep relationships with people around you. It is also possible to only be preaching the gospel to the natives, but not to be living like them or having meaningful relationships with them. It is important to be doing all three of these: preaching the gospel, cultivating deep relationships with the locals, and living like the locals. This book is not about how to preach the gospel in a cross-cultural environment, nor how to build deep relationships with those around you. It is just about the aspect of becoming like the native in all other aspects of life.

This balance is similar to what Paul says to the church in Thessalonica, that "he loved them so much that he was delighted to share with them not only the gospel of God, but his life as well" (1 Thess 2:8). So Paul desires to share with them not only the gospel, but his life as well. This book aims to help with the part of ministry that results from truly sharing our life with the local people, particularly in regards to becoming like them.

Paul's Words Related to Contextualization?

Many people in the evangelical missions circle for the last few decades have been talking about the word "contextualization". What exactly is contextualization? David Sills describes it "simply as the process of making the gospel understood."[1] This definition is very broad and does not necessarily include just the message itself. Elsewhere contextualization is defined by Scott Moreau as "taking the gospel to a new context and finding ways to communicate it so that it is understandable to the people in that context."[2] So contextualization is presenting the gospel to people in a way that they can accept it. This presentation of the gospel is not just related to the verbal message of the gospel, but all other parts of the missionary's life. It's the other parts of the missionary's life that this book is about, how the missionary can better relate to the locals in all aspects of life.

Paul's words very accurately define contextualization: "to become all things to all men so that some may be saved." This is the essence of contextualization. Paul will go to any length in order to better present the message of the gospel. Paul desires that those around him will see him and trust him because of how he loves them and cares for them, and he shows that through his demeanor, appearance, and all aspects of his life. There has been much focus in other books on how to contextualize the message of the gospel to different peoples; this is not what this book aims to accomplish. In fact, the message itself is just one part of contextualization. The other part is how the locals view the messenger. The locals' perspective draws from all other parts of the messenger's life, and not

---

1. Sills, *Reaching and Teaching*, 205–7.
2. Moreau, Corwin, and McGee, *Introducing World Missions*, 12.

just the message itself. This is the part of contextualization that this book is about.

Questions to Discuss

1. In your context right now, to whom are you trying to minister? Are you intentional in trying to reach those near you with the gospel?
2. Whether serving as missionaries abroad or living in your hometown where you grew up, how are you trying to be intentional to become all things to those around you that they may be saved?

2

Must Have Humility and Love

Humility in Becoming All Things to All Men

BECOMING NATIVE TO WIN the natives is not just a matter of outward appearance and saying the right things. Maybe the biggest part of becoming native is the missionary's heart itself, rather than anything on the outside. The missionary must put on a spirit of humility even to begin to be brought low enough to be used by the Lord to reach a foreign people. First we must look at Christ's humility and how we can imitate that. After that, we will look into the example of Paul's humility in reaching those he ministered to.

Philippians 2:5–11—Humility in Christ Becoming a Man and Being Crucified

The concept of becoming all things to all men requires some amount of humility on the part of the missionary. We can understand the idea of humility through Paul's writing on Christ's humility (Phil 2:5–11). Christ, though being in nature God, humbled himself by making himself nothing and coming in the form of a servant and a man (v. 7). And not only that, but Christ humbled himself by taking on the most shameful and humiliating of all deaths—death on a cross (v. 8).

At that time, death by crucifixion was the most humiliating and degrading form of death possible. And it wasn't just Jesus as a normal man who died in the most shameful way possible. It was that same Jesus Christ that the Apostle John described in this way: "The Word was *with* God and the Word *was* God" (John 1:2). So the Almighty God Incarnate, the second person of the Trinity, Jesus Christ, was not only mocked and scorned and spat on, but he was killed in the most demeaning and disgraceful manner possible.

And this is the model of humility that Christ set for us. Not only that, but Paul emphasizes the humility of Christ and that we as mere humans are to imitate that unbelievable model of humility.

Philippians 2:3–4—Considering Others' Interests above Our Own

In the context of Paul's writing about Christ's humility—in fact right before the verses above—Paul talks about not doing anything "out of selfish ambition or vain conceit," but in humility to "consider others better than [ourselves]." We are not to "focus on our own interests, but on the interests of others" (Phil 2:3–4). These are practical examples of how we are to imitate Christ's humility. Thankfully, as we are weak sinners, the power to fulfill these words comes not through our own strength, but rather through the Holy Spirit combining with the Word of God to convict and mold our hearts, gradually making us more and more like Christ.

So in thinking about imitating Christ's humility by thinking about others' interests above our own, it is critical that we model an attitude of humility as we try to minister cross-culturally. There are many reasons in cross-cultural communication to feel very proud. Maybe we move to a new country that is much poorer than our country, and we are constantly thinking about how the new country is not as good as our home country. The people are not as well educated as where we come from. The roads are not as nice.

Must Have Humility and Love

The train stations are much more crowded. The restaurants aren't as clean as where we come from. The people are not as cultured as what we are used to.

Here's an example of something that happens every day when walking down the street in China: a woman will spit on the sidewalk or send a snot rocket plummeting to the ground while walking her grandchild home. If we were in our own country, this would be considered completely unacceptable and disgusting behavior for anyone, especially a woman. But in China, that is not the case. A woman here does not lose any respect from others by hocking a big loogie on the sidewalk for all to see. We could feel anger at seeing such things, but instead we are to love people even when their cultures are completely different from ours.

In China, it is also very normal for people to cut in lines. This is hard for Westerners to stomach, as we are used to the clear protocol in our countries that lines function according to the principle of "first come, first served." So we think ourselves civilized as we stand and wait in an organized manner, but in China—maybe because there are so many people everywhere, and people have had many bad experiences of being shut off a bus—people are not generally too concerned about lines.

When waiting at the train station to get train tickets, it is pretty normal for people to try to jump to the front of the line, while everyone else has been waiting an hour or more in that line. We get very offended by it, but we can pray that the Lord would give us great patience to love such people who do things that are just not acceptable in our home cultures. Being able to love those who should offend us is right in line with the humility that Christ exemplified in his life. We are called to consider others' needs above our own. That is what humility means. So in regards to living in a new culture, we must constantly remind ourselves, as my missions professor Dr. David Sills said in my seminary class, "It's not right. It's not wrong. It's just different."

In missions, we are called to have a spirit of humility in such a manner that we consider others' interests above our own. We must not believe that our interests are supreme in the universe; rather we should manifest a selfless and caring attitude towards others through the work of the Holy Spirit.

Genesis 13: Abraham Considering Lot's Interests above His Own

We see another example of considering others' interests above our own in the story of Abraham and Lot's separation in Genesis 13. Quarreling was arising among Abraham's men and Lot's men. It was clear they needed to go in separate directions. In verse 9, though Abraham was the elder and thus should have had the first choice of land, Abraham deferred to Lot and let him choose the best land. So Lot chose the land he wanted, and Abraham got what was left over. This is a great picture in the Old Testament of what Paul says in the New Testament about "considering another's interests above our own" (Phil 2:3–4).

Abraham, in this story, was living out the humility that Paul talks about Christ modeling in Phil 2:5–11. Though the original context of Paul's words are about humility shown in the church to other believers, many of the same principals of humility are required in cross-cultural ministry. We are called to love the people we are with, together with their culture. That means that we are not to dwell on and groan about the bad conditions and cultural differences of the people and place we are reaching. When we do this we are only thinking selfishly about ourselves and what we need, rather than about the interests of those we are trying to reach. We also hinder the spread of the gospel. Who wants to hear about God after you have berated someone about their behavior and told them they are doing life wrong, or rolled your eyes toward someone in disgust?

It takes great humility to use the concept of "putting others' interests above our own" in a cross-cultural setting. In order to apply this concept, we must not cling to our cultures and values as though they were absolute truths. A popular example of this may be when we as Westerners, who are generally punctual in arriving places and getting things done, move into a new cultural setting where punctuality is not valued at all, like in South America, Africa, or many Muslim areas.

In our minds we can cling to the fact that punctuality is a biblical and right trait, when in fact this quality is mostly related to our backgrounds rather than any absolute truth. So we must humble ourselves, take off our watches, and adapt to the new culture by trying not to get so bent out of shape by things related to time. We must accept the culture and values of our new home. We must prefer their interests above our own, which in this case means seeking to follow their cultures and values more than our own.

Rather, we are to follow Abraham's example by not being consumed by our own interests, but thinking about the interests of others. We cannot simply think about all of the things we are lacking and how the new place does not have a McDonald's. If we are consumed by our own needs and grumbling about where we are, then it will be impossible to love the locals and to be concerned about their spiritual needs. We will simply be grumbling in self-pity against God. So we must put on humility by forgetting about all the reasons we should hate the local culture and place, so that we may become more like them in order to reach them with the gospel, that they may turn from darkness to light.

Romans 12:1-2—Imitating Christ's Model of Self-Sacrifice

Along the same lines as the idea of "putting others' interests above our own" is the model of self-sacrifice in the life of Christ. We see how Christ laid down his life for us, setting the ultimate example of humility and love. In the same way are we called to "offer our bodies as living sacrifices, holy and pleasing to God, this is our spiritual act of worship" (Rom 12:1-2). We are called to imitate Christ's example of self-sacrifice. Our lives are no longer our own. We are to lay down our lives before Christ and ask him what he wants us to do with them. This is similar to cross-cultural ministry, as we must in some sense put to death parts of the culture that we come from, as a sort of sacrifice to the Lord. We must then in humility take on a new life in the new culture, being open and obedient to how Christ wants to use us there.

Mark 8:34—Denying Ourselves, Taking Up Our Crosses

Elsewhere Christ says that if we want to follow him, we must "deny ourselves, take up our crosses, and follow him" (Mark 8:34). This is very similar to the example above. In cross-cultural ministry this means to deny our needs and habits from our own cultural background, for the sake of following him and making his gospel known to the locals. So we can see examples from Christ in what it means to deny ourselves for the sake of following him and knowing him better. The focus in this book is on denying the comforts of our own cultures in order to love those from a completely different culture, that they may come to know the Lord.

The model of Christ above is what we are seeking to follow, in order that we may not just be warm bodies in that place, who have no heart for the people. Rather, may our hearts be warm with love and humility for those around us. When constantly dwelling on all of these shortcomings of our new home, it is easy to feel proud about where we come from, that we in some sense are people of privilege who just happen to be living in an inferior land for the time being. If we have such thoughts, then it is impossible to become like the natives to win the natives.

In order to become like the natives, we must learn to love their culture and their country. If we are to love their culture and country, we cannot have a critical attitude of them. If we just want to grumble about what a bad place it is, then it will be completely impossible to love the locals and strive to become like them. When we have this complaining attitude, it mostly stems from pride in our own home country and a feeling of disgust against those we are trying to reach in the new land. In order to really dive into the culture and people, it is necessary to have a spirit of humility about us, to accept and love them and their culture for the good and the ugly.

We must make an intentional effort to resist the temptation to complain about that place. Though it can be incredibly challenging sometimes to love the local environment, we are to strive to have a humble and loving attitude towards the locals and our new culture. We are to deny, in some sense, the impulses of our minds and hearts that want to hold on to our home culture and reject the new place. Only through the power of the Holy Spirit can we do any of these things.

Love in Becoming All Things to All Men

Just like humility is necessary in becoming all things to all men in cross-cultural ministry to win some, in the same way an attitude of love is equally important. If we cannot love those we are ministering to, we are essentially wasting our time in trying to reach them. Love means that we care intensely for their greatest good. Love means that we not only talk about making deep relationships with those around us, but that we actually walk in love and do it. Many missionaries, before they are sent out, have ample training and understanding of the concept of loving those in the place they will go. It seems like something that will just naturally happen once they arrive there. But oftentimes, after arriving in that place, it is a whole different story. It can be incredibly challenging to love the people around you. This is the case especially when the place is dirtier and noisier than your home country. Plus you initially cannot speak the language, and even trying to go to the grocery store or hospital to get anything done is a huge headache. Let us look to Christ.

Matthew 14:13–15—Christ's Love for Others

The ultimate model for us as far as love is concerned is the model of Christ himself. In chapter 14 in the book of Matthew, King Herod has just gruesomely beheaded John the Baptist (vv. 1–12). In verse 13, Jesus hears about John the Baptist's beheading and withdraws by boat to a solitary place, probably to mourn what had happened to his cousin and friend John the Baptist.

But if Jesus was looking to escape the crowd for a spell to grieve alone, this is not what ended up happening. Rather, the crowds heard where Jesus was and followed him by foot from the towns. I think we can all imagine the scene here, particularly how we would feel if we were Jesus in this situation. Sometimes we just need to have some alone time away, especially if we are having a time of mourning or loss. It would be terribly frustrating in that instance to have people chasing after us if we just wanted to be alone to grieve. Even more so, Jesus simply wants to mourn the terrible death of his beloved cousin and friend. Is that too much to ask? But he could not even get enough privacy to do that. I know if I were in his situation and a crowd was following me, I would be terribly upset and overwhelmed and just want to disappear or run away from that place forever.

But what did Jesus do in this story? Verse 14 tells us that when Jesus landed and saw the large crowd, he had compassion on them and healed their sick. To me, this story is a sweet picture of Christ's love for the people. Even in the moment when he could have been the most hateful and resentful towards the people for following and bugging him when he was trying to grieve the loss of his good friend, Jesus had compassion on them and healed their sick. What great love and affection did Jesus display for these people!

This is a model that we are to strive to imitate in cross-cultural ministry, to follow the love of Jesus for the people. We admit we are incredibly weak to follow such a model, especially in situations like this where the last thing we want to do is to love the locals around us who may be doing something that should annoy us. Thankfully we have the Spirit of God inside of us to mold us and make us more Christ-like.

If we want to think about examples of Christ showing love to others, we do not have to think too hard. In fact, it would be a safe assumption that, since Jesus never sinned or hated anyone, therefore everything he did towards others was done in love. This was the case even when he spoke harshly to the religious leaders for their hypocritical hearts or spoke sternly to people, urging them to repent and turn to God. He loved them because he cared first and foremost for their greatest good, which was that they might know God. So the example above was just one of many examples showing Christ's love for others. But any other story about him could also be used to show his love.

When we claim to be believers, but we do not treat people in a loving manner, we are acting hypocritically. It is very similar to the religious leaders of Jesus' time, who claimed to know God but in fact had wicked hearts with no true faith. It is similar when we are in a foreign place, and we claim to be followers of Christ, but we act very ugly and critically toward the locals. They must see us and think that Christians are not loving people. Obviously this is not the message we want to convey.

So we must keep in mind, as people in a foreign land are seeing our behavior, that we are representing Christ to them. Hopefully we are properly representing him, rather than giving him a bad name. Of course none of us wants to be compared to the hypocritical Pharisees, but sometimes even we, as believers, are like them—only concerned about ourselves and not loving toward those around us. In such cases, we shall pray fervently that the Lord will renew our hearts and change us from the inside to be able to love those in this foreign place.

Paul's View on Christ's Love

Elsewhere Paul talks about the love of Christ in regards to his crucifixion for sinners. Paul says, "While we were still sinners, Christ died for us" (Rom. 5:8). This is the greatest example of love that we can fathom. We see this also in Ephesians 5:1–2, as Paul writes that we should "live a life of love." Paul continues by writing that our love should follow the example of Christ, who "loved us and gave himself up for us as a fragrant offering and sacrifice to God."

In cross-cultural ministry, in an effort to become "native to win the natives," we are to follow the model of Christ, particularly in how he loved us. We are to imitate his love for us. Christ displayed sacrificial love for us when he died on the cross. We are to love those around us sacrificially. We should lay down our lives for them. That is quite a challenging model to follow. Sometimes it is hard enough to even tolerate those around us in a foreign country, much less to like them or even love them. It's much easier to just make fun of them and talk about all of the negative things about the place and the people there. In such situations, love for the people does not just come naturally. How are we, as mere men, able to love like this?

Paul's Example of Love

Paul was a normal guy, but he set an extraordinarily high standard for how to love others for the sake of saving their souls. Paul was not a perfect and sinless man like Jesus. Jesus was the only man who ever lived as a sinless man. Jesus was the Son of God, so though he was tempted like we are tempted, he never fell into sin. On the other hand, though he was an apostle and minister to the Gentiles, Paul was still just a normal guy. Paul's life included many sins, probably even daily struggles with sin. Paul was a sinner not only before his conversion but also after his conversion as well, just like we are.

Though he never mentioned it in his letters, I'm sure Paul also had times when he struggled to love people like Christ loved them. I'm sure at times he would feel frustrated about how he had a critical attitude towards those he was ministering to, rather than a loving attitude. Paul was a mere mortal man like us; hence, he struggled with things that all people struggle with. That said, we can still learn a lot about Paul and his love for those he was seeking to reach. As far as what he wrote in his letters, he sets a high standard for us to follow. And probably Paul was not able to follow his own words completely, but still was often failing in obedience to what he knew was right. Nonetheless, we can strive to follow Paul as a mortal sinful man who truly loved those around him and saw many of them saved and transformed by the gospel.

Must Have Humility and Love

1 Thessalonians 2:8—Paul's Love for the Believers

In Paul's letter to the church in Thessalonica, he writes, "We *loved you so much* that we were delighted to share with you not only the gospel of God but our lives as well, because *you had become so dear to us*" (1 Thess. 2:8). This is particularly impressive because when Paul wrote this letter he had only spent a few weeks together with the church in Thessalonica. Nonetheless, he writes about his abounding love for them. This is a model that we are to strive to imitate, that out of abounding love for the locals we are really sharing our lives and faith with them.

Philippians 1:8—Paul's Affections for the Church

To the church in Philippi, Paul writes, "God can testify how I long for each of you with the affection of Christ." (Phil 1:8). Here Paul expresses his love for them in writing. His affection for them is so strong that he compares it to Christ's affection for them. It is possible to spend time regularly with people without actually having strong affection for them. It is even possible as a minister of the gospel to be ministering to people and to not have strong affection for them. This is entirely possible! But we are not to let our affection for the people we are ministering to ever wane or dim. We should wrestle in prayer and strive for a heart that is changed by the power of the Holy Spirit to have affection for the people that we are taking the gospel to. If we do not love them, how can they accept the witness of Christ's love that we are preaching to them?

Romans 15:16—Paul's Burden for the People

We must also have a huge burden for those around us as we seek to minister in a foreign land. We can see the huge burden of Paul for the Gentiles, as he was "a minister of Christ Jesus to the Gentiles with the priestly duty of proclaiming the gospel of God, so that the Gentiles might become an offering acceptable to God, sanctified by the Holy Spirit" (Rom 15:16). So everything Paul did was for the sanctification of the Gentiles, to present them as a holy and fragrant offering to the Lord.

Here, Paul is not just talking about going and living around a group of people; Paul is talking about love. Paul is imitating the love of Christ for his church. These are not just natural affections that stem out of being around people. Actually such affection is incredibly hard to conjure up on one's own, even impossible. Such affection for the people only comes through the work of the Holy Spirit in us that helps us to sacrificially and radically love those around us, even in a foreign land. May we cry out to the Lord to have mercy on us, to give us huge hearts for those to whom we are ministering.

Questions to Discuss

1. Are your relationships with those you are surrounded by characterized by an attitude of love and humility towards them?
2. Are you constantly praying to the Lord to give you a humble and loving heart towards those around you?
3. Do you find yourself easily becoming critical of those you are trying to reach? In what situations?
4. Do you ever just have a feeling of hatred or great frustration towards the local culture you are in? What makes you feel that way?

Section II

Practically How to Become Native to Win the Natives

3

Diving into Language

The first section of this book was about *principles* in "becoming native to win the natives." The second section of the book is specifically how to *carry those principles out*. So, we understand what the Bible says about what we should do, but what exactly does that look like in practice? And what should we strive to make important if we are to reach those we are ministering to cross-culturally? The first thing to look at in striving to become like the natives is the sometimes scary and intimidating—but also incredibly fulfilling and worthwhile—process of learning the local language.

Language Learning

Learning a foreign language is not necessarily the easiest thing in the world to do. Since I first arrived in China ten years ago, people back home have always asked if I was "fluent" in the language. But I think fluency can be described in many different ways. I thought after my first year in China that I was relatively "fluent," because I could pretty easily use Chinese to do most things I needed to do around town. But as each year passes, I realize that for my first years in China I still could not understand very much compared to how much I can now. And I'm sure that if I stayed here for another five years, I would probably look back at my Chinese level now and see how low it is, comparatively. So "fluency" is a very relative term.

In language learning, though, especially when living in the country where the language is spoken, it is important to be satisfied with making slow and steady improvement. Many foreigners come to China from all over the world to learn Chinese. They will study incredibly intensively for about two years until they pass their desired level of Chinese. After that, they may never really learn much more. But for those of us who are missionaries, we need to have a long-term view in sight.

We are not just learning the language to pass an exam. We are using the language to convey who God is. That is one noble task. The language is a means by which we can better connect with the local people for ministry purposes. Everything we do in learning the language should be very practical, as that is the way we can connect better with the locals. Through better connecting with the local people, we can better share with them about the gospel of Jesus Christ. So we must have these things in mind when we learn the language. We must be satisfied with slow and steady progress, which over a long time can amount to great language mastery.

For the missionary, we must have more of a marathon mindset when studying the local language, rather than a 100 meter race pace. Our purpose in studying the language is not simply to pass an exam. That does not mean that if we just stay in a foreign country for long enough we will just naturally become a language master. That is certainly not true. There are many missionaries who live in a country for decades, but never learn the language well. The only way to learn a language well is to expend much sweat and effort to learn it. There is no other way to do it. It will not just happen naturally. But especially for a missionary, the sweat shed for this cause is well worth it.

Intense language learning is certianly not for everyone. For older missionaries who are beyond a certain age, it is not wise for them to spend hours upon hours in learning the language. It can be a huge waste of time for them to do that, as with their old age it can be incredibly difficult or impossible for most to learn a new foreign language. Such older missionaries should not feel at all discouraged with that reality. Thankfully, in probably nearly every ministry context out there in any country, there will be locals who can speak English well. Thus, the older missionaries can minister to them, which is also of great importance. But for those young enough to learn the local language, it is well worth all of their efforts to learn the language as well as they can, and to continue indefinitely to improve their language.

For those of us from the United States, foreign language learning is not something that just comes naturally. In fact, though the United States' education system is quite excellent in most regards, in regards to learning foreign languages it is behind much of the rest of the world. Most people from non-English speaking countries begin learning foreign languages like English and other languages from a very young age. And they put enough emphasis on language learning that they can actually learn it well. I know when I was in middle school and high school in the United States, I studied Spanish for several years, but despite having very good grades in the class, my Spanish level was still very low. I could not even have conversed with someone in Spanish then.

Standardized college entrance tests in the United States like the ACT or SAT do not require anything related to a foreign language. Even many majors in universities in the United States do not require any foreign language classes, or they accept credits from language classes taken in high school. The GRE also does not include a foreign language section. For those of us who are from the United States, we come from a culture that does not emphasize learning foreign languages. So when we first go to the mission field in a foreign land, we do not immediately know how we are to learn the language. It can be very intimidating in many ways, because we have never attained any level of fluency in a foreign language before. We do not know how we are to begin the language-learning process, nor do we know what steps to take beyond that in order to come to any mastery of the language.

But if you plan to minister in a foreign land, it is very likely that English will not be the main language where you are serving.

If English is not the first language there, then you still can probably find some people around you who speak English well enough to become your friends. You may even study the Bible with them in English and minister to them in English. Certainly there is great need in many unreached areas around the world for people to minister in only English to the locals. That said, if you plan to spend more than a couple years in that country, and you are young enough to somewhat efficiently learn a foreign language, it would greatly help you to learn the language as well as you can.

Even in more educated countries, only a small percentage of the general public will be able to communicate fluently with you in English. So that means that if you never learn the local language, you'll only be able to communicate with a small portion of the population. This will greatly limit the scope of your ministry. But if you can be diligent in studying and learn the language well, oh how many doors will open for building deep relationships with locals and for sharing the gospel with them! They will also greatly respect you for caring about their culture by working hard to learn the language. If you do not make any effort to learn their language, they may think you really do not like their culture and their country. Like I said, it is possible to do cross-cultural ministry in only English, but even with the good English speakers there will be limitations so long as you cannot speak to them in their heart language.

Not only is the best way to communicate with people in their mother tongue, but the language is also a great way to learn more about the culture. There are just so many things that are learned about a culture through the language itself that cannot necessarily be learned by being translated into another language. One fun thing also is to try to learn some of the local dialect in the town particular to where you are serving. The dialect there may be very different from other parts of the country. So a fun way to relate to the locals there is by learning some of the more common local phrases and using them with those around you who are from there.

Diving into Language

In language learning, it is important not to be terrified of making mistakes. You must be brave to go out and talk to shop owners or restaurant workers or to buy veggies in the market. It's completely fine if you mispronounce a word terribly or say the wrong thing. The most important thing is that you are willing to open your mouth to try to communicate with those around you. If you are too afraid to speak and make mistakes, you will find it very hard to make progress in the language. The mispronouncing will happen less often if you have ten people correct you and remind you how to say a word correctly than if you never open your mouth to be corrected.

I remember how funny it was—at least to us at the time—when my college friend Eric, who initially moved with me to China, told me about how he had made such a stupid mistake when trying to ask for a napkin at a local rice restaurant. He meant to ask for a *canjinzhi* (napkin). But instead he asked for a *sanmingzhi* (sandwich). He felt quite silly when he realized his mistake, especially since the restaurant had nothing on the menu resembling a sandwich. He was good-humored about his mistake, and we had a good laugh about it later. Though he was certainly embarrassed for his error, it didn't stop him from getting out and continuing to practice his Chinese with anyone he would see.

It seems that for the Chinese language in particular—because of the ambiguity intrinsic to a tonal language—it is quite normal for the locals to sometimes be very confused about what the foreigners are trying to say to them, even if the foreigner has been living there for a long time. Is the foreigner saying "Mom," "horse," "numb," or just cursing you? These are four of the possible meanings for the simple word *ma*, all with a different tone. And even beyond that, there may be fifty common characters with completely different meanings just for the word *shi* (pronounced close to "sure") with a falling tone.

So it's understandable in learning any language to have some miscommunications or mistakes. The key for the language learner is not to be afraid of making such mistakes, but to persevere in trying to speak as much as possible with the locals. That's the only way to improve in the spoken language. If someone has learned a language to some extent, but cannot or will not actually speak it to have a conversation with a local, what is the point of learning the language? The whole purpose for a missionary to learn a language is to converse with the locals so as to be able to befriend them and as a means of sharing the good news with them. The only way to practice conversing in a foreign language is to open one's mouth to talk with locals.

Language Learning Tips

As for my own language-learning experience, many folks study the language full-time for a couple years before doing anything else. I was never a full-time language student, but rather a full-time English teacher. But after I had arrived in China, I immediately had a great interest in studying the language. At first I tried to memorize simple conversational words, and my vocabulary slowly broadened. My second semester in China I began studying Chinese characters. I enjoyed this even more and started to spend about fifteen to twenty hours per week just writing and reading characters. I did that for another two years. During that time, even when I was on holiday in the United States, I'd still continue to try to study Chinese characters for at least twenty hours per week. This helped give me a great foundation in the language, though I was not a full-time Chinese student.

Around the same time, I began listening to the Chinese radio and writing down all of the words I did not understand and trying to look them up. Also, during my third year in China for a whole year every morning I would wake up early and read aloud for an hour from the Chinese Bible. This really helped not only my speaking, but also my Chinese character recognition and my spiritual language vocabulary. In my third year in China I started making good friends who did not speak any English. All of our correspondence together was in Chinese, and we would talk about relatively deep topics. Another way to improve my language skills was to have a regular Chinese Corner with a couple of my other foreign and Chinese friends. We would get together twice per week and just chat together in only Chinese for a couple hours. This was a terrific way to practice our oral Chinese, plus to have opportunities to minister to the Chinese friends who would join us.

Chinese standardized tests have also been a way to push me in the language. I've taken the standardized Chinese exam (HSK) twice. In 2009 I passed level 5 in the HSK. In 2011 I attempted the highest level, HSK 6, and failed by eight points. Whether passing or failing, a great thing about taking the Chinese standardized exam is that it forced me to practice the parts of the language that I may otherwise ignore. For example, I previously spent tons of time studying Chinese characters and slowly improving my oral Chinese, but one thing I never studied closely was Chinese grammar. In preparing for the standardized Chinese exam, I was forced to study all the most detailed Chinese grammar rules. Obviously grammar is an important part of learning the language, but it was something I was not too strong in before. After having to study the grammar rules for my exam, my language skills became much more well-rounded.

When studying a language, it is important to constantly remind yourself why you are doing it. Studying a language is not just in order to pass exams. It is not for the end goal of simply being able to share the gospel with someone, but not be able to talk about anything else. The purpose of language is to be able to better love the people. If you are more invested in learning the language, you show the locals how much you care about them and their culture.

So it is important in language learning to make sure to have some component that requires you to actually interact with the locals. So that means that you do not just want to study the language alone and never use it to make local friends. You also do not just want to be in a classroom with other foreigners learning the language together. Of course it is important to study language on your own, or maybe to be taking a class to help learn the language, but that should just be one component of learning the language.

You need to make it a priority to always have some consistent way to use the language to interact with locals. Maybe that means simply trying to use the language as much as possible on a day-to-day basis with anyone you come across. Maybe that means you have a local language tutor who meets with you regularly to teach you the language. Having a local language tutor is not only a great, practical way to use the language with a local, it is also a great way to develop friendships that lead to opportunities to share your faith with them. Another way to consistently use the language with locals for the purpose of building friendships is to volunteer at a local restaurant, which I will cover in the next section. If you go there every day, those who speak the language will surround you, and you can use the language to build deep friendships with those around you in hopes of sharing your faith and life with them.

So one should not just think about learning a language simply as a way to pass an exam or satisfy the basic requirements of your organization. Rather, it should be something you enjoy and see as a road to greater serving the Lord. So in language learning, it is not only important to memorize grammar rules and vocabulary lists and to study by using textbooks or by being in a classroom. Though all of these are important, your language learning experience will serve its purpose if these are the only ways you practice the language. You should strive to be using the language with locals regularly, with hopes of building true friendships with them and trying to share your faith through that.

Volunteering at a Local Restaurant

A way to connect with the locals better is to volunteer at a local restaurant or shop. By doing this, you may significantly improve your language, while also building relationships for outreach. You may wonder how one would go about doing this. Well, first you need to think about a place that you really enjoy going to where you already have some familiarity with the boss. Then you or a local friend can just ask the boss if it would be okay if you started coming in about five to ten hours per week to help them out. You don't need any salary. You tell them you are doing it because you want to learn more of the language.

Diving into Language

In the middle of my first year in China in 2005, I started volunteering at a nearby Chinese rice restaurant called Red Eagle. Since I was already teaching at the university, I didn't volunteer at Red Eagle in order to get money. I would work at Red Eagle about fifteen hours per week. I would wipe off the tables and carry the dishes around. Although they did not give me any money, they would occasionally give me free food, which was a blessing because it was the best restaurant on the street. I volunteered at Red Eagle for about fifteen hours per week for about a year.

At that time, as it was my first year living in China, my language skills were pretty minimal. But just being in an atmosphere at Red Eagle where everyone around me was always speaking Chinese was really helpful. The boss and other workers couldn't speak any English. Neither could most of the customers. So I would just hang around there, help out a little, and soak up the language and try to learn as much as I could. I worked at Red Eagle for about a year. Often after lunch at Red Eagle, I would jump rope or use the hula-hoop or kick the Chinese hacky sack outside with the other workers.

Certainly they appreciated me because I could help attract customers by showing my foreign face there. At that time, as my Chinese level was very low, I could not converse with the workers about my faith too extensively. However, I was able to give a couple of them Bibles. And some of my close Chinese Christian friends were able to share with them about their faith much more fluently than I ever could have. So there is great value in trying to volunteer at a local store or restaurant, even if your language level is not too good.

Volunteering at a local restaurant or shop is not only good for rookies in the language. Currently, in my tenth year in China, I am now again volunteering at a local Chinese restaurant, this time at a breakfast place I call "Waffle House" (don't be fooled—waffles are not on the menu). They serve Chinese breakfast: tofu custard, hot soy milk, eight-treasure porridge, small rice porridge, hard-boiled eggs, Chinese funnel cakes, and Chinese pancakes. Though I have now been in China for a long time, volunteering at a restaurant keeps me improving my Chinese, not to mention building deep relationships in the community for the purpose of outreach.

One way doing this helps is in regard to steady language improvement. As I've never been a full-time language student, I seek rather to maintain consistent and diligent language study over a long period of time, seeing slow, steady progress over the years. So volunteering at Waffle House for five to ten hours per week now helps me to continue developing my language skills. Also, while working at Waffle House I can speak with the workers about the city we live in. I can learn much more about Chinese culture, history, and customs, as I spend many hours just sitting and chatting with the other workers and customers.

Now, since I have been in China much longer, and because my language skills are much farther along than that first year in China working at Red Eagle, I am able to talk much more extensively with the workers, and I am also able to share my faith more clearly with them. This year for Easter, for instance, I was able to give the other four workers each a copy of the Chinese Bible and tell them that my faith is the most precious thing in my life. Since that time, I have slowly had doors here and there to share more about my faith with them. They can see my character—how I work hard, how I have a humble spirit in working there for free, and how I interact lovingly with them and the customers. So I pray that as I am able to slowly share with them about my faith, some of them may come to know the Lord.

It is also a great way to meet folks in the community for the purpose of ministry. There are people from all backgrounds who go there. Many workers at my high school eat there. So I can just hang around there and chat with those who come in. It can really deepen my relationships with them. I can get to know a huge number of people who live in our area. One older man, Mr. Gao, who was a customer when I first started working at Waffle House, would come every day for breakfast, and we slowly built a relationship. Now I eat with him one-on-one every week. He is still not a believer, but I gave him a Bible and have shared with him extensively and am able to share with him weekly about the Lord.

The only way I ever would have met him was through working at the Waffle House.

Earlier this semester I met another person of note who was eating breakfast at Waffle House. During our couple years living at the high school, we had often prayed that we would be able to meet some in the neighborhood who were believers. We thought there must be some house churches in the neighborhood, but we really had never even heard of anyone in our neighborhood that was a believer. This changed through an encounter at Waffle House with Brother Ma.

I was near the end of my shift at Waffle House when an older man asked me to sit down with him and chat, which is not too uncommon. Like many Chinese, he asked me why I did not open a private English school to make more money. So I thought that was all he wanted to talk to me about. But after some basic chitchat, I realized that he'd gone to school in Hong Kong. But he didn't just go to a normal school in Hong Kong, he went to a *shenxueyuan*, which is a seminary. I was completely amazed.

Then he told me that not only is he a believer, but that he and his wife lead a house church in our neighborhood. I couldn't believe it! He also owns a local business that helps pay for the house church's needs. I can confidently say that I never would have met this Brother Ma if not for working at Waffle House. It just allows me a presence in the community, because all kinds of people walk through the market daily and eat at Waffle House. Sometimes I get impatient, thinking that I am not connecting enough with the Waffle House customers. But I must be patient, and the Lord will put people in my path.

The average Chinese person I come across at Waffle House is quite amazed that I volunteer there. Generally speaking, having such a job is reserved for the lowest-class people in China. So they are shocked to see a teacher like me wiping the tables and the plates, or cutting off a square of tofu for them. The Chinese culture is very concerned about the concept of "saving face" and doing everything to not "lose face". In Chinese culture, for a teacher like me to be cleaning the tables, they think I should be concerned about losing face. They are impressed when I seem to have no concern about losing my face.

They think that I must have some spirit of humility in me to be able to work hard doing a job like I do at Waffle House just for the sake of trying to learn the language better. In most countries around the world a foreigner would be welcomed to volunteer at a local restaurant for the sake of language improvement and reaching the people. It may be worth thinking about it if you have any spare time to do this. I just go to Waffle House in the mornings whenever I'm not at class or between my classes. Even just volunteering five hours per week can go a long way, regardless of where your language level is.

Questions to Discuss

1. How has your experience been as you've learned the local language? What are some strengths and weaknesses of your language learning?
2. How have you been able to integrate language-learning with actually being with locals, rather than just studying in a classroom alone?
3. Would it be possible where you are to do a part-time volunteer job at a local restaurant for the sake of language improvement and opening doors for ministry?
4. What are the possibilities for studying language in the country you want to go to? Who can you connect with to explain the possibilities in that country?

4

Assimilating into the Local Culture

One way to really show care and concern for the locals is to have a genuine desire to learn more about their culture. If we show a real passion for their local culture, it will make it easier for them to relate to us and trust us. There are many aspects of the local culture, like history, food, language, music, and entertainment. All of these things combine to make up the heart and worldview of the local community. If we really dig into these various cultural aspects, the locals will respect us more and welcome us in with arms wide open. They will no longer see us as an outsider. They will see us as one of their own, which makes it easier for them to accept the message of salvation we bring to them. So, what are some ways, culturally, that we can strive to become more like the natives, so that some may be saved? Well, just think about all aspects of their lives and how to make a conscious effort to try to do the things they do.

Sports

Consider what the locals do in their free time. I am fortunate now because I live in a country where my favorite sport is the same as the most popular sport for young local men: basketball. I can bridge many gaps with locals by talking with them about basketball and the NBA. For some of you, your favorite sport may not be popular in the country where you are serving, but you may still find a place where you live to play that sport and meet some locals who also like it. Or maybe you can try to learn the most popular local sport, be it badminton or cricket or soccer or something else. This may be another way to dive into the culture to become like the natives to win the natives.

Local Music, Movies, and TV Shows

Another cultural way to relate to the locals better is to take some time to learn about what kind of local music is popular for people your age. Certainly, as long as it does not have incredibly crude or immoral lyrics, it can be a great way to learn about the culture (and the language). For example, in the United States I would never enjoy listening to pop music. But I enjoy Chinese pop music and like to keep up with the latest artists. My favorite Chinese pop stars include (unfortunately not international stars yet): Jay Chou, Wang Leehom, and Fang Datong. Going to Chinese karaoke (KTV) is a common pastime for Chinese people. I went regularly at the beginning of my time in China. I learned to sing many of the Chinese pop songs, and even my wife and I would on occasion stay home for date nights and sing Chinese pop songs together, looking up the lyrics and playing the music on our computer. Learning Chinese music has been a great way to help win the hearts of the locals.

And when the Lord gives us opportunities to spend time with the local Chinese believers, we are able to learn more about the Chinese praise and worship songs and sing them together with the Chinese. This is a great way to connect with the local believers. It is also a picture of heaven as we see those from every tribe, language, people, and nation worshipping the Lord and singing praises to him. It is great to be familiar with the culture of the local Christians where you are, including their songs. This is best done through spending as much time as you can with local believers.

Watching local movies and TV shows is also a good way to learn more about the culture and practice the language. Recently my wife and I have enjoyed a somewhat new Chinese reality show called "Dad, where are we going?" It is a fun way to learn about the family dynamics in China and parenting from their perspective. Also, it is a great way to strike up conversations with locals, because it seems that nearly all Chinese people of various ages and backgrounds enjoy watching that show. It also helps us to practice our Chinese listening and to learn more colloquialisms. In your own context you will need to filter out which shows are available to watch for your family, and which shows should be avoided. Ask your friends, and tell them carefully what kind of shows you do not enjoy and you would not want your family to watch.

Holidays

Wherever in the world you serve, learn about the local holidays, and if possible try to celebrate them with your local friends and their families. The Chinese people put a huge emphasis on their traditional holidays: Spring Festival (Chinese New Year), Dragon Boat Festival, Tomb Sweeping Festival, Lantern Festival, and National Day, to name a few. Ask your local friends about the most important festivals in your country. Try to learn as much as you can about them. When the time comes to celebrate, get together with your local friends and when possible do what they do for the festival, whether that be eating the special food for that festival, going to visit their relatives, or setting off firecrackers. This is a great way to experience the local culture and to connect with the locals by enjoying and celebrating their holidays.

Also, it is fantastic if your local friend invites you to his or her home for the holiday. You can see your friend's family and celebrate the holiday in someone's home. You can learn about the family environment and family dynamics in that country. In China, for the Chinese New Year, relatives will give each other a red envelope filled with some money. If you go visit a Chinese friend's home for the Spring Festival, then probably their family will try to give you a red envelope filled with money. It is okay to try to refuse it a few times, but you must eventually accept it. This is the case even when the family lives in an incredibly poor farming village and they have almost no money, while you have plenty of money. Nonetheless, you must still eventually accept the money so that they may save face and be considered good hosts.

Celebrating festivals with locals can also be a good way to have open doors to share the gospel with them. For example, in China everyone in the family will usually go to the local Buddhist or Taoist temple for the Spring Festival to burn incense and bow to the idols for good luck for the New Year. Obviously you don't want to participate in anything that will compromise your faith in Christ like burning incense to or bowing to idols, but it is a good opportunity to at least walk around the temple with your friend and his friends or family and to try to ask him about his religion. This is a great way to look deeper at your religion with your friend or to talk about it for the first time.

In China, for the Tomb Sweeping Holiday in the spring, all people over about thirty years old will buy fake money and light it on the streets. They say that they do it because all the fake money they burn will go up to their ancestors in the afterlife. If you really dig in deep and ask if they really truly believe this, most will say that they don't really believe it but that it is a superstition. Their ancestors burned fake money to their ancestors, so your friend is obligated to do it, too. That said, it is a great opportunity to talk about our belief in the real afterlife and our true inheritance in heaven, one that is not shaken or destroyed.

Transportation

In trying to better relate to the locals in order to win the locals, one simple way is to consider which kind of transportation they use and to try to follow them in that. For example, in our current city in Northwest China, most people take buses around the city. My first few years in China, I almost never took buses; I always took taxis. I did not even know the bus routes around the city, though it was a smaller city.

Assimilating into the Local Culture

Very rarely do you see foreigners riding on the buses. Usually they just don't go anywhere, or they take taxis to get around, or they buy their own car. A good way to better relate to the locals here—not to mention to save lots of money on taxi fares—is to get a bus card and try to take the bus everywhere. The trips will be a little longer, but usually not unbelievably longer. It will not only save you some money, but you may be able to talk to locals on the bus. There is also benefit in being able to relate to the locals even a little bit more, by being able to really understand what it is like to take three busses to get to the other side of the city for work and make the return journey back home every evening.

In the same regard, instead of taking planes to visit other cities in your country, consider taking the trains. Just like with the busses above, it is a great way to be surrounded by common folks. Trains really are a great way to meet people. Depending on the condition and newness of the trains, they could be either very nice or pretty smoky and stinky. Nonetheless it is a cheaper and more culturally enriching way to get to other cities around you. In China, if it is a long train ride, you can get a bed instead of a seat. That way you can sleep the whole trip and wake up at your destination feeling refreshed. I've never experienced that when taking an airplane!

Also, as trains usually have many people and usually have a very social atmosphere about them, it is a great way to meet folks. In is very possible even in the span of a train ride to be able to speak with those around you about spiritual things. Just a couple months ago I was talking with some local folks on the train and the topic of religion came up. Through that, I was able to share a little bit about my faith. We continued talking about Christianity for quite a while, and one of the older men listening admitted that he had started the train ride very skeptical of my words but finally was touched and interested to know more about the good news I was proclaiming.

Food & Drink

Try your best to slowly adapt your diet so that it is more like that of the people you are ministering to. In regards to diet, I am thankful to live in China, because the food here is wonderful. The rice and dishes, the various kinds of noodles, and the Chinese dumplings are all fantastic. Each region of China has very distinct foods, so in each city there are different kinds of restaurants representing all of the different cuisines found around China. It is hard to run out of new things to eat here. It is possible to buy nasty things in China, like scorpion on a stick, stinky tofu, or other things of that nature—certainly such things are not too appealing to me and I have no problem saying no to them—but as far as the common food of the people, try to adapt to eating it.

Usually for foreigners in a new country it will take a little while for your stomach to adjust to the new food. If you get very sick of the local food early on, just keep pushing through and pray that you may soon enjoy it. Being able to eat the local food that others make for you, or that you can buy at a local restaurant or food stand, is a nice way to honor the culture that you live in. If you only eat American food in your home or only go to foreign restaurants and stores, then it will make it harder for you to relate fully to the locals and for them fully to accept you.

When I first arrived in China, I thought it very strange that the Chinese would almost always prefer a hot drink to a cold drink. In all seasons other than summer they will even drink a glass of just steaming hot water. In the United States, we're used to drinking cold beverages throughout the year. Even in the winter in a cold place, it's not too uncommon as an American to go inside a restaurant to find refuge from the cold, only to order a large coke with ice cubes in it.

When I first arrived in China, I thought that drinking freezing drinks in the winter was a very normal and reasonable thing. I thought the Chinese had it wrong in rejecting the cold drinks. But slowly I realized that the Chinese locals' comments that the hot water in the winter is "good for your digestion" actually makes much more sense than the American drinking iced cokes in the middle of the winter. In such instances, when we realize that it's actually our home culture that does things weird, not the new culture, maybe we should consider adopting the local custom.

That's what I've done with drinking glasses of steaming hot water in China.

On another note related to drinks, on the topic of drinking alcohol or not, you should do what your conscience tells you to do. Some organizations forbid their missionaries to drink even a drop of alcohol. Personally I have no objection to alcohol drinking in general. There is nothing in the Bible that says all alcohol drinking should be forbidden. Paul says, "Everything that is done without faith is sin" (Rom 14:23). So if you have doubts about drinking alcohol, you are sinning if you drink it. If you have no doubts about it, then you are okay to drink some as long as you are not drunk (Eph 5:18). And you also must not drink any if it causes other believers around you to stumble because of you (1 Cor 8:13).

Personally, though drinking alcohol in China is a huge part of the culture, I just tell those around me that I do not drink alcohol at all. They may ask me to only drink one drink, but I know that after that they will continue to ask me to drink more. At some point I would need to say no anyways, so I may as well say no at the beginning. Also, all of the mature Chinese believers that I have met have completely sworn off any kind of alcohol, maybe because of the huge influence of alcohol on men in the Chinese culture. So I think that if I were drinking any alcohol for any purpose, even in small doses, it may cause Chinese believers to stumble. They may think it disappointing when they consider that I, their foreign friend who they thought was a mature believer, am now drinking alcohol, which mature believers I have relationships with in China do not do. Maybe where you are serving you may also come across some of these same questions and situations. May the Lord grant you his wisdom in such cases.

Vacations

When you get any periods for vacation and you are not traveling home, consider traveling to other parts of your country, either to visit your local friends or to explore the country. It is of great benefit to better understand the country you live in, and a great way to do that is to travel around to different places in the country. This also forces you to develop your language skills; when traveling, you must regularly interact with locals to be able to get around.

During my decade in China, I have had several opportunities to take long trains to visit other parts of the country. We can travel from place to place by train. I have had several trips, of at least a month each, just traveling around different parts of China. Some of the places we would visit would be to stay with local friends. We could visit their hometowns, and they could show us around the area. Some places we would visit because we had heard about them and wanted to see them first hand.

Whether we travel with other foreigners or with Chinese friends, traveling is terrific for deepening bonds with those you are traveling with. Because I have traveled to so many areas around China, I feel like I have a pretty good understanding of the different cultures, places, and people in different parts of the country. Also, when I meet Chinese people in my city who are from other parts of China, I usually have at least some sense of their hometown and have maybe visited there or a place nearby. China is a big country, so I still feel like there are many more places here I could travel.

Questions to Discuss

1. Whether in your hometown or living abroad, do you make any effort to be like the people you are around, that you may better reach them? How could you do this better?
2. Would the people you are around describe you as being "distant" from them in cultural ways, or as being culturally close to them?
3. What do the normal people with your age and job like to do in the country where you serve (entertainment, sports, music, food and drink)?

5

Appearance to Local Community

ONE IMPORTANT THING ABOUT ministering in a place is how the people in that community view you. This is quite important and can sometimes be overlooked or underestimated. This has several different factors, including your physical appearance, your job, and whether the locals view you as a legitimate person in the community. If most of the people in the community see you as a shady and suspicious character, then it is very likely that they will be hesitant to believe any message that you tell them about your faith; so pray and think about exactly what that will mean for you as you minister to the locals. How can you fit in with those around you and be a contributing person within the local community?

Physical Appearance

One aspect related to ministry is our outward appearance. As I mentioned before, Hudson Taylor set a good example to follow when he put away his foreign clothing and hairstyle and adopted the local Chinese clothes and long braided hair. This was a big part of why the locals welcomed him and why they were more open to listening to him. He did not stick out anymore to the local people as a foreigner. Rather, he looked like the locals did. And that is why they so readily welcomed him in. So how does this apply today?

Practically How to Become Native to Win the Natives

Well, it is important to look at those around you. You should probably aim to dress like those around you who are of a similar social status, age, and salary as you.

I can give an example from our modern times: Certainly it is no longer fashionable in China for men to have a long braid. For the most part, they do not dress too differently than us foreigners. But there are subtleties in their appearance that can be noticed. For me, I used to always wear my hoodie around, as it is comfortable and pretty normal for Americans to wear hoodies. As I spent time with Chinese people around my age, however, I realized that none of the Chinese men in their young 30s would wear hoodies. So, in trying to fit in better with the culture, I stopped wearing my hoodies around outside and just wore sweaters or collared shirts like the Chinese men.

I cannot say that any locals have been saved as a result of me not wearing hoodies outside anymore, but it seems that any small steps we can make to be more like the people are well worth it. We never know what small adjustment can play even a small part in local people trusting us more because they think we look more like them than like outsiders. When the locals trust us more, they will be more open to hearing the message of hope we desire to proclaim to them. Another way to accomplish the above is to try to purchase local brands of clothing, rather than relying on people from the United States to send you clothes. Wearing the local clothing is another way to fit in with the people and to have camaraderie with them.

Here's another example of fitting in with the local dress: As I teach in a prestigious high school, I used to feel like I needed to dress formally, with slacks and a collared shirt or sweater. Particularly, I felt like this would be the appropriate way for a young, male high school teacher in the United States to dress. Oddly enough, though, as I looked around at the young, male, Chinese teachers at my high school here, I noted that, surprisingly, they did not dress nice at all. In fact, I see many of them wearing tennis shoes, windsuit pants, and a sweatshirt to class. It still surprises me to see so many of the young Chinese male teachers wearing this outfit. It

Appearance to Local Community

just did not seem right. I continued to persist in wearing my slacks and nice shirt to class.

Recently, though, I wanted to experiment with trying to dress like the young, male, Chinese teachers do for class. So I wore jeans, a collared shirt, and my nicest tennis shoes. I felt so uncomfortable going into the building in such informal attire, but when I walked into the classroom the Chinese students seemed to be completely comfortable seeing me in such informal clothes. And when I looked at the young, male, Chinese teacher who is in charge of those students, he was wearing the exact same thing as me: jeans, a collared shirt, and tennis shoes. I will need to push through the mental barrier that makes me think I am just being a slacker when I dress like that to teach and seek to fit in better with those in the same occupation and age as me, even if that means being a bit different than such a person with the same occupation and age would be in the United States.

Also related to appearance is one's facial hair. In college I often had a beard, but when I first moved to China and grew out a beard, I realized that no one around me had a full beard. So, for the most part, I have remained clean-shaven while in China. That said, I do know that as Hudson Taylor got older and remained in China, he grew out a very long beard, which I am sure made him stick out from the locals, as most Chinese people cannot grow beards. In many Muslim countries, it may be normal for the local men to grow out a mustache. This would be a great opportunity for the missionary men to grow out a respectable mustache of their own.

Here's another example related to body hair: At the end of my second year in China, I stayed in my city during the hot summer while all of my foreign friends were gone. I noticed that many locals—even strangers on the bus—would touch my arm or leg hair and comment on how long it was. Feeling some annoyance after several times of this happening, and having lots of time on my hands, I decided to shave all of my arm and leg hair, in an effort to look more like the locals. I found life to be very comfortable in the summer that year, and I was no longer shocked anyone on the public bus with my long arm or leg hair. I could now go about my business without anyone harassing me.

Job

Another aspect of our appearance to the locals is the job that we have in that city. Especially in closed countries, it is not possible to be a full-time "missionary" on a "missionary" visa. So if you want to live there, you have to be a legitimate worker or student in that country and have the appropriate visa for that. Our job is a way that we can contribute to the local community, and it is a way for us to build friendships for the sake of outreach.

When I first arrived in China ten years ago, I was twenty-two years old and just out of college. Somehow, with nearly no qualifications or experience, I was able to get a job teaching English at a university in eastern China. During my first years teaching in China, I had the attitude that teaching was a means to an end. In other words, my purpose in living in China was to do missions, not to teach. Also I had to have some kind of visa to stay in the country, and teaching gave me a visa to stay in the country. So, I thought that teaching gave me a means to have a visa and stay in the country to be able to do ministry.

But with that attitude, I put almost zero importance on the job itself. I would put no effort into the teaching, and sometimes I would even make up lesson plans as I was walking to class. I had no concern in my mind about trying to be a decent teacher, other than to try to arrive to class on time and wear a collared shirt or sweater. It was not until several years into my time teaching in China that the Lord helped me realize the importance of the job itself. It is not simply a way to get a visa to stay in the country; rather, it is an identity within the community. It is what I put my hands to, and thus I should aim to do it as well as I can.

Paul talks about this in his letter to the Colossians, that whatever we do, we are to "work at it with all our hearts, as working for the Lord and not for men, since we know that we will receive our inheritance from the Lord as a reward" (Col 3:23–24). I still do not consider myself to be a naturally-gifted English teacher. My wife is much more of this than I am, as even outside of class she is thinking about how to improve her classes. For me, when I'm not in class I am not thinking about specific ways to improve the class. So, in that regard, I would not say I have a passion for just the teaching. But, athough I absolutely hated teaching English for my first several years in China and put no effort into it, the Lord has now helped me to enjoy it and to put in all the work necessary for the teaching. And hence I can aim to be an outstanding teacher, rather than just seeking to fly under the radar and get by.

Integrity in the Community

The last aspect related to our appearance does not necessarily have to do with our physical appearance, but rather with how we appear to locals. What I mean is that it is important to consider how the locals will view us in their society. For example, if we are a full-time student or have a low-paying job, but somehow we can afford to live with our family and multiple kids in the wealthiest apartment complex in the city, the locals will be very suspicious about us, particularly in closed countries where official missionaries are illegal.

The only way into closed countries is through other visas and legitimate jobs. Often missionaries are supported financially by donors back home or through funds from missions organizations or churches. It is a question of integrity. If the locals wonder where this person got all the money to live a luxurious life, and the foreigner doesn't have the job to back it up, certainly the locals will be suspicious.

It is necessary in any culture around the world that someone must work to get paid and buy things. But how come the foreigners are able to live luxurious lives with large families if their only source of income is a low-paying job—if they even have a legitimate job? It seems too good to be true. The locals must suspect that the foreigners are engaged in some kind of illegal activity, like missionary activities or working for the CIA or trafficking drugs.

Practically How to Become Native to Win the Natives

So, it is important for the foreigner to live according to his means, to live in an apartment that appropriately corresponds to his salary in that place. Otherwise, the locals will be suspicious and it could be a huge barrier for sharing the gospel with them. If they cannot trust you and what you stand for, then you have nothing.

I mention this because it's certainly an issue for many workers around the world in many different organizations. It seems to be the norm for missionaries to live relatively lavishly, well above the foreigner's local salary. One way to become like the locals to win the locals is to live lives like they live, to blend as well as possible into their culture. This is also related to how you spend your money, and whether your standard of living fits your income.

One thing to mention briefly on this topic is that some missionary families have multiple children, and thus it is necessary for them to live in the nicer apartment complexes because they have such a big family and need a big home. This seems to be reasonable, especially for those with a big family. I know that in China, because the younger Chinese families are not allowed to have many children, the apartments have fewer bedrooms. So only in the most expensive apartment complexes is it possible to buy three- or four-bedroom apartments to accommodate larger families. It seems reasonable that in such circumstances large missionary families live in nice apartment complexes with more bedrooms.

On the same topic, there are some missionaries whose purpose is not necessarily to do outreach to the people living near them. For example, there may be a missionary whose purpose in being there is to train local pastors in theology. If this is the case for the missionary, probably he will need to focus on this important ministry full-time, so it would not be helpful to have a full-time job.

Living in a closed country, it is still necessary that such missionaries have a visa to live there. Often it is much easier for such missionaries to have a long-term student visa that allows more flexibility for the missionary, but for those who intend to reach those in their community, it is best to have a legitimate job and a work visa. After studying the language full-time for a few years in order to be a legitimate part of the local community, it is important to have some kind of real job. Many missionaries will go to great lengths not to get a job. They will stay on a student visa for ten years or more, even though they do not even go to the classes anymore. It seems it is much better to have a student visa while full-time language study is really happening, then to try to find a job as a platform to the ministry.

If someone has been in the country for a long time and they have a large family and nice apartment, but have only been on a student visa and never worked, that is incredibly suspicious to the locals. Again, this is a question of integrity. If the locals are suspicious about your salary and living standards, is there any way that they can trust you? If they cannot trust you, are they likely to listen to any of the things you tell them about Christ Jesus? Probably not. We must seek diligently to live lives of integrity in the local community.

Questions to Discuss

1. Do you take much effort to look like the people around you? How could you do that more?

2. Wherever you are and whatever you do for your work, are you properly "working with all your heart as working for God and not for man"?

3. How do you think people view you in the community you live in? Do you think your lifestyle (home, car, things you buy) helps your witness for Christ or hurts it?

6

Family Life

MISSIONARIES WITH KIDS CAN face many more challenges on the mission field than singles or those without kids. Unless the kids are born in the mission field and spend most of their childhood in that place, there will be many difficulties that come from living with kids in the mission field. This will be the case regardless of how old the kids are. If the kids are teenagers when you move to the mission field, they may have even more intense difficulty adjusting to living in that new place, as they were probably much more adapted to living in their home country. If the kids are quite small when moving abroad, the adjustment process should be a little faster. Usually the younger the kids are, the faster they can adjust to new things and surroundings.

Kids' Education

As far as the kids' education is concerned, especially in larger cities, there may be many different options. One option is for the kids to just go to local schools full-time, even as they get older, with everything being in the local language. This is the best way for the kids to master the local language and make local friends. A negative would be that the parents might not necessarily agree with everything their kids are learning at the local school. Another option is to do homeschooling. This may be a way for the parents to spend more time with the kids and have a greater influence over them in their education and upbringing. This option would also be much cheaper than going to international schools. A negative would be that they wouldn't have as much interaction with other kids. Also, it may be harder to learn the local language.

Many cities also have international schools that are quite expensive but can provide a solid education. Such schools usually have kids from all over the world, and may have few or no local kids. These schools may be at the same level educationally as a good school in the United States. Some potential downsides of the international schools are the cost and, possibly, less interaction with local kids.

It seems, from all the interactions we have had with missionaries with many kids, that if the parents desire their kids to learn the local language well, it is best for the children to attend the local schools for at least half-days for as long as possible. In China, the "kindergartens" begin at three years old. So, as our daughter turned three years old this year, we found a local kindergarten to put her in. She goes Monday through Friday, from 8 a.m. to noon. It is a great way for her to learn Chinese, and she can make lots of local friends. Our daughter loves the local Chinese kindergarten so much that often when we go pick her up after the morning, she doesn't want to go home with us but wants to stay at the school for the whole day. The missionary children should enjoy being around the local kids and be able to communicate with them in their language. The best way to do that is to put them into the local schools or kindergartens, at least for a while.

I have heard before that a child can learn a new language easiest before they are seven years old. That is true, and a child in that age range can learn languages very quickly once in an environment to do it, like a local school where they only speak the local language. That said, it seems that as quickly as the child under seven years old can pick up the language, so will he also lose the language if he is taken out of that atmosphere. So it is important to leave the children in the local school as long as possible, at least for half-days.

Another model is to have the children in the local schools for a half-day, and homeschool them for the other half of the day. That takes a big commitment from the wife, though, to homeschool the kids, and it is not necessarily a great option for every family. In China, it seems normal for missionary families to put their kids in the local schools for half-days, at least until they are about ten years old. If the child at this age has been in the local schools for many years, probably they have mastered the local language well enough that it will stay with them as they grow up.

However, it seems that if they just learn the local language for a few years when they are very young, probably the language will not stick with them when they grow up. Either way, once the child is taken out of the local schools—whether to homeschool full-time or to put them in an international school—if they have already learned the local language pretty well, it is important to help them continue to be surrounded by the language by facilitating continued play with local kids or trying to speak the local language more at home as a family. This will be necessary when the child is not full-time in a local school surrounded constantly by the local language.

And if you stay in the foreign country for long enough, there's a good chance that your family will make adjustments over time about what works best for your family at that time. Maybe you will start with the mindset to only homeschool, but will later change to a local school or international school. And maybe some of your options will vary according to what kind of city or town you live in and what kinds of education options are found there. Certainly the children's education is something that each family must decide on their own. What may be great for one family may not work well for another.

Medical Care

Another part of family life abroad is medical care. If a missionary family or just a single missionary lives overseas long enough, it is inevitable that needs for medical care will come up. Those can be quite stressful, as the missionary may be quite comfortable getting medical care in his own country, but pretty clueless about getting medical care in this foreign country. If the medical issues are related to the missionary's children, then it can be even more stressful. It's one thing when the missionaries are suffering, but when their kids are suffering it takes the situation to a whole new level of anxiety and urgency.

So, with that being said, in dire situations many missionaries in recent history have left their cities to go to a larger city nearby, or even back to their home country, to get medical care. This is quite reasonable. When a loved one is in urgent need and is suffering physically, the family wants to do everything in their power to make sure that their loved one will receive the best care possible, and often the best care is not possible in the city where they serve, so they go home or to another nearby country in order to get medical care. Maybe a mother desires to go back to her home country to deliver a baby, so the family will all go back together for several months while the mother delivers the baby. Again, this is very understandable and may vary according to the family's situation.

Though it is quite nerve-racking when medical care is needed in a foreign country, I have found that depending on the local medical care is something that is a great way to show trust in the local country and people. As long as the medical care where you live is not awful, it may be good for you to stay where you are to have your baby, or to have surgery or other medical care. Many missions organizations will take their workers out of the local city to deliver babies in nice hospitals in other nearby countries. Though this may be the safest way to receive medical care or have a baby, it may be a hindrance to the work, not only by removing the family from that place for several weeks, but also by showing in some sense a lack of trust in the local health care.

We had our oldest daughter in our former small Chinese city, in a small hospital with only Chinese-speaking doctors and nurses. And it was a great experience for bonding with the locals, as they saw that, in having our baby there, we were putting a lot of trust in them and their medical care. They respected us because we went through exactly what they went through when they had a baby or needed medical care. Our experiences were the exact same in our times of need, and that bound our hearts together. People who leave the city or country to have a baby can really miss out on that bonding with the locals through the means of common experiences.

Several years ago, I had a surgery in my small Chinese city, also with all Chinese-speaking doctors and nurses. I felt I was blessed to not go do the surgery in another city or country, though that was my first instinct. While I was in the hospital, many of my local friends were able to come visit me and help take care of me, which helped build bridges between us. If I had had the surgery elsewhere, those friends would not have been able to help me out, which would've been a missed opportunity to grow closer to them and increase our mutual love and trust for one another. Also, before I left the hospital after my weeklong stay there, I was able to write Chinese letters to each of the doctors and nurses to thank them for taking good care of me. In the letters I wrote some Scripture verses and the basics of the gospel. I also gave them Chinese Bibles before I checked out. This experience of being able to share my faith with the workers at the hospital was even better because I was sharing with those who lived in my city, who were my neighbors.

Outreach as a Family

The main reason for a family to move to a foreign country is to do outreach to the locals. But outreach is not to be done just by the father. The whole family, including the wife and the children, should do outreach together. That means the whole family needs to make an effort to try to enjoy the place and love the people, which sometimes takes a little while. Typically, the wife may have the hardest time adapting to the missions field, as she may feel burdened taking care of the kids most of the time. And maybe the husband is studying the language or working full-time while the wife must stay home. It is important that the husband can encourage his wife in living in that country.

One question is whether the family should become missionaries if only the husband or the wife—but not both—have the desire or calling to be missionaries. We know the example of William Carey, who became the father of the modern missions movement when he jumped on a boat to India in the late 1700s. His wife did not have the same calling as him. Nonetheless, they went together to India, and she eventually went crazy there and remained in that state for many decades. The question is, if Carey had decided not to go because his wife did not have the same calling, would all of his years of fruitful service in India have happened?

But I think we can all agree that it is better for both the husband and the wife to share the same calling to go. Sometimes, though, the husband loves the place while the wife hates it, or the other way around. I shall not attempt to try to answer the question of whether both the husband and wife should be equally called to a place to serve. The point is that the missionary family must strive very hard to be united in the ministry, to not compete against one another or have resentment against one another.

The husband in particular, as the leader of the family, is responsible for the physical and spiritual well being of both his wife and the kids. If they are not adjusting well to being in the mission field, the husband is responsible for encouraging them and for helping them love the locals. If the wife hates the local culture and people, then pray that the Lord would change her heart to love it. Generally speaking, the children will see the local culture however their parents do. If the parents make fun of the local people and seem to hate the culture, then the kids will probably do the same. If the parents love the local culture and people, then the kids will usually do the same. If the parents strive to fight through cultural boundaries to love the local people, then the children will do the same. If the parents do not do this, then their children will not either, and they will resent and hate the locals.

Often it is the families who have recently arrived in the foreign land that find it the hardest to love the locals. One reason is that adjusting to a foreign land is generally much harder for families than it is for single folks. Oftentimes, though the family is very excited to be moving to that place after praying for a while about it and feeling great confirmation from the Lord to do so, once the family arrives in the foreign land it can be incredibly challenging. In such times, maybe the hardest thing to do is to love those around you. It is much easier to simply be critical of everything about that new place.

Wife's Language Learning

The wife also must be encouraged to try to learn some of the language to be able to get around and buy things and meet locals. The wife's language acquisition may be much slower than the husband's if she is taking care of the kids full-time, and that is okay. Some missionary families are encouraged by their organizations for the husband and wife to both study language full-time for two or three years. In many cases this is not just for the husband, but for the wife as well. So, the husband and wife both study the language thirty hours per week for two or three years. That means that the children are not being taken care of by their dad or mom. They may hire a local lady to watch the kids for thirty or forty hours a week. This goes on for a few years. I do not agree with this approach. Certainly the wife's language skills in this situation end up much better, but it does not seem worth it.

For a few years someone outside the family is raising the kids. It seems that the damage done to the kids' and parents' relationship in this situation is not worth it. It seems more reasonable to expect that the wife will slowly study the local language and the husband will study full-time, while the wife puts more of her attention on taking care of the family. For her, studying the language should never be a higher priority than taking care of her family.

When these priorities are mixed up, it can cause much havoc in the family.

Questions to Discuss:

1. Whether you live abroad or at home, how is your family a part of your ministry to the people around you? How could your family be more a part of outreach?
2. If you serve abroad, is your family's situation ideal there? What are some things you would change about it?
3. If you're not married yet, what would you like your potential future family serving abroad to look like?

Section III

What to Take Away from All This?

7

Final Thoughts

What if You Don't Love the People?

FIRST AND FOREMOST, IF you realize that the only thoughts and words that you have about the place where you now live are critical and negative, be reminded that you are actually having a very normal experience for foreigners who move overseas, even those who are moving overseas as an ambassador of Christ. Do not feel like you are a completely unloving and callous person. Do not think that you are a complete failure as a missionary, or that you have wasted your time and money to move overseas to try to serve the Lord. Certainly these critical and unloving thoughts towards the locals are not pleasing to the Lord—that is definitely true—but it is also important to recognize that the Lord is patient with us. Even when our sin is obstructing us from serving him properly, he still is patient with us. If we seek him, he will guide us in serving him and loving others.

Also, we must remember that we are still an unfinished work. In other words, the Lord is slowly purifying us day by day further into Christ's likeness. That's what Paul tells us in 2 Corinthians 3:17–18, that "we are being transformed into Christ's likeness with ever-increasing glory, which comes from the Lord, who is the

What to Take Away from All This?

Spirit." So, though we may be unloving and critical towards the locals today, that does not mean that our whole experience living in that place will always be like that. The Lord desires to change us more into his likeness each day, and if we are true believers, we have the Spirit inside of us that *will* transform us. Also there just tend to be seasons in which we are more or less critical of the locals. If we realize that we are in a season in which our hearts are hardened towards the locals, we can pray that the Lord would pull us out of that season.

It is very common when living cross-culturally to just have a real challenge in loving the people you are around. More often than not, it is the people who have lived in that place for less than a year or two who will struggle most with not having much love for the locals. But this can also be a problem for those who have been living there for much longer. Maybe earlier in your ministry you had great love for them, but now you have noticed that this love has slowly dimmed and waned, and you just find yourself being very critical of them—this also happens from time to time. So, what are some ways to turn away from your critical and harsh attitude towards the locals? And how can you turn towards loving them and having great affection for them?

Well the first thing to do is to pray to the Lord. Pray to him for repentance—to repent that you simply find your heart very unloving toward the local people. Ask that the Lord would forgive you of these sins. Pray that the Lord would give you a huge heart for the people, that you may be able to love them like Christ does. Pray that the Lord would have mercy on you that you may understand deep in your heart that those people are lost without Christ and destined to eternal life in torment, separated from Christ.

A burden for the people should not come from mere guilt that you are not doing the right thing, but it should come naturally as a result of your intimate relationship with God. Pray fervently that the Lord may give you great affection for the locals. Maybe even spend particular time looking through the Scriptures to find verses that talk about God's or Christ's love. Then pray through those Scriptures, that the Lord's mercy may be on you to love those around you in the same way. It may be good to take a meal or a day for fasting, to not eat anything, but to spend particular time in prayer to the Lord, crying out that he may soften your heart toward the locals.

Another very simple way is to be more intentional about making deep friendships with some of the locals. If you only have surface-level acquaintances in that place, but no true friends, it will be much easier to be critical of the people and the place. So one simple and practical way to better love the locals is to pray that the Lord would give you a genuine friend in that place, then go and interact with people. Maybe you have someone in mind that has been cordial to you, but you have not taken any further steps to really befriend him or her. If that is the case, go and see them and chat with them more. Get their phone number and try to keep in touch with them and see them more regularly. Pray that the Lord would give you great affection for that person.

Generally speaking, if the Lord gives you a local friend whom you really love and care for, then you will no longer be focused on how bad the place is where you are living. Suddenly, your relationship with that person, and the hopes and prayers that they may come to know the Lord, will become much more important than your previous problems with the local culture and people.

Objectively Analyzing the Culture

All who've lived or traveled abroad would agree that one thing that results from living in a foreign culture is not only an understanding of the new culture, but also a better understanding of one's own culture. It is important to evaluate both our new culture and our home culture with a biblical lens. We can understand that there are some positive and negative aspects of both our own culture and our new culture.

What to Take Away from All This?

Local Cultures' Positive Aspects Worth Imitating

One positive aspect of the local Chinese culture is that most Chinese people are incredibly patient compared to westerners. Most Chinese people have spent the majority of their lives waiting in huge lines to get on trains, busses, or do other things, so they've developed a great ability to wait for things without grumbling and complaining. But if a westerner has a thirty-minute flight delay, he will feel as though the whole world is crumbling. This includes myself. We as westerners are generally not patient. But every year, many Chinese must wait for a few days, sleeping at the train station, just to get tickets so they can sit or stand for thirty to fifty hours on a train to visit their relatives for a couple weeks for the Chinese New Year. So in this regard, the Chinese peoples' patience follows much more closely the biblical teachings about patience.

Another thing that westerners can learn from the Chinese is their observance of filial piety—the concept of obedience to one's parents and elders. Typical westerners shun such ideas, as we intensely value independence and individual freedom. It seems strange to us that most elderly Chinese folks live with their kids and grandkids. The grandparents often play more of a part raising the grandkids than do the parents. To a westerner, it seems too constrictive to have all three generations—grandparents, parents, and grandkids—all living together long-term under one roof.

The Chinese explain this by saying that they do this because they need to "repay" their parents for birthing them and helping raise them. For us westerners, it doesn't seem right to do something just as a repayment, particularly to our parents. But that's actually exactly what Paul writes in 1 Timothy 5:4, that we are to take care of our parents and grandparents to "repay [them], which is pleasing to God." So, again, the Chinese culture in this regard is actually much closer to following this biblical standard than is western culture.

Final Thoughts

Local Cultures' Negative Aspects Must Be Rejected by Missionaries

On the other hand, anything about the local culture that is anti-biblical or cannot be reasonably adhered to should not be followed. For example, in Chinese culture, sometimes the husband and wife will work in different cities from one another for long periods of time—even for decades. They do this so as not to compromise their careers. For Chinese, providing for family means to make as much money as possible. This is the case even if that means the father lives and works long-term in Beijing while the mother lives and works in Guangzhou and the kids live in Shanghai with their grandparents.

This is quite common for Chinese families; essentially the parents will only see their kids a couple times per year and have no real relationship with them. This may be the way of life for the children's entire upbringing. The parents are seen as doing the right thing because it means they can make the maximum amount of money to best "provide" for their family. This is of greater value in Chinese culture than actually living with your wife and kids and having a real relationship with them.

The above scenario is very common in China. When we as Christians see this, we should recognize that it is not according to the biblical standards of what it means for the father to properly lead his wife and kids. So we as Christians should not follow these trends within Chinese society, because they oppose what the Bible says about family.

Some practices in your local culture will just be strange to the westerner, and thus very hard to follow. An example of a Chinese custom in China that western missionaries don't necessarily need to adopt is the practice of Chinese women taking a month of rest (*zuoyuezi*) after their baby is born. This idea doesn't go against the Bible in any way. In fact, the Bible doesn't mention anything about it. But it is such a strange practice or superstition that it would just be nearly impossible for western women missionaries to follow. For the first month after the baby is born, the woman stays inside for about forty days, with all windows closed and air conditioning off. They cannot shower, watch TV, read a book, or touch water of any kind.

The grandma is in charge of taking care of the mother. The belief is that if the mother opens a window or breaks the rules at all during these forty days, then she will suffer later in her life with arthritis or other ailments. So the Chinese women follow the rules because their mom wants them to and because they are terrified that they may be stricken in some way physically later in life because of their neglect during the forty days after having the baby. So some local cultural practices are worth imitating, while others are not. A foreign female missionary could be respectful of this custom, though, even if she doesn't follow every rule exactly. She could take more time inside to rest and relax and spend time with her baby and family during that first month. She could limit the amount of time spent outside and be watchful of wearing enough clothing if/when she does venture out during that first month. These things can help to show that the woman is taking care of the body God gave her and also taking care of the child God has created.

Conclusion

For each of us who serve cross-culturally in another country, we must constantly check with ourselves about how our attitude and love is developing towards the locals. We do not aim simply to live overseas as warm bodies that have no real, eternal impact on the locals with whom we live. Rather, our prayer is that many locals may be drawn closer to Christ because of our time and service in that place and among those people. The ultimate model of humility and love we follow is that of Christ, who humbled himself to live as a man and humbled himself to die in the most humiliating and shameful way possible—a death on a Cross.

A couple of men who have followed Christ's example of humility and love towards the locals were Paul, and Hudson Taylor. Paul's love for the Athenians in Acts 17 and Hudson Taylor's model of ministry with the Chinese show us what it means to "become all things to all men, that by all possible means we may save some" (1 Cor. 9:22). May the Lord's mercy be on us, that we may humbly and lovingly dive in with the locals, to go to all reasonable lengths to live like the locals, that it may impact even a single person to better trust us and more easily trust the God we serve.

Questions to Discuss

1. How are you being active in loving those around you?
2. Whether living at home or abroad, have you prayed to the Lord to forgive you for a lack of love to any around you?
3. Are you crying out to the Lord to give you a spirit of love and humility to those you are ministering to?

Bibliography

Moreau, Scott A., Gary R. Corwin, and Gary B. McGee. *Introducing World Missions: A Biblical, Historical, and Practical Survey.* Grand Rapids, MI: Baker Academic, 2004.

Sills, David M. *Reaching and Teaching: A Call to Great Commission Obedience.* Chicago, Moody, 2010.

www.ingramcontent.com/pod-product-compliance
Lightning Source LLC
Chambersburg PA
CBHW070100100426
42743CB00012B/2604